ONCE UPON A TIME IN FRANCE, a baby was born under the summer sun. His parents named him Jacques.

As he grew, Jacques fell in love with the sea. He dreamed of breathing beneath the waves and swimming as gracefully as a fish. In fact, he longed to become a manfish.

Jacques Cousteau grew up to become a champion of the seas and one of the best-known oceanographers in the world. In this lovely biography, poetic text and gorgeous paintings come together to create a portrait of Cousteau that is as magical as it is inspiring.

Praise for Manfish: A Story of Jacques Cousteau:

★ "Poetic . . . lyrical and concise. . . . Puybaret's smooth-looking acrylic paintings extend the words' elegant simplicity and beautifully convey the sense of infinite, underwater space." —*Booklist*, starred review

★ "Moving . . . This poetic profile of a doer and a dreamer is certain to inspire fresh interest in discovering, and in caring for, our world's wonders." —*Kirkus Reviews*, starred review

"Almost poetic in its rich descriptions, the text is superimposed on ethereal acrylic paintings, submerging readers in the marine world." —*School Library Journal*

"A colorful and evocative picture of one man's long love affair with the world below the waves. . . . It would pique the interest of young ocean enthusiasts." —*The Bulletin of the Center for Children's Books*

A New York Public Library Recommended Reading selection

A Nick Jr. Magazine Best Book

A Book Links' Best New Books for the Classroom selection

A Junior Library Guild selection

A Booklist Online: Top 10 Sci-Tech Book for Youth of the Year

An IRA Children's and Young Adults' Book Award Winner

An IRA Teachers' Choices Reading List selection

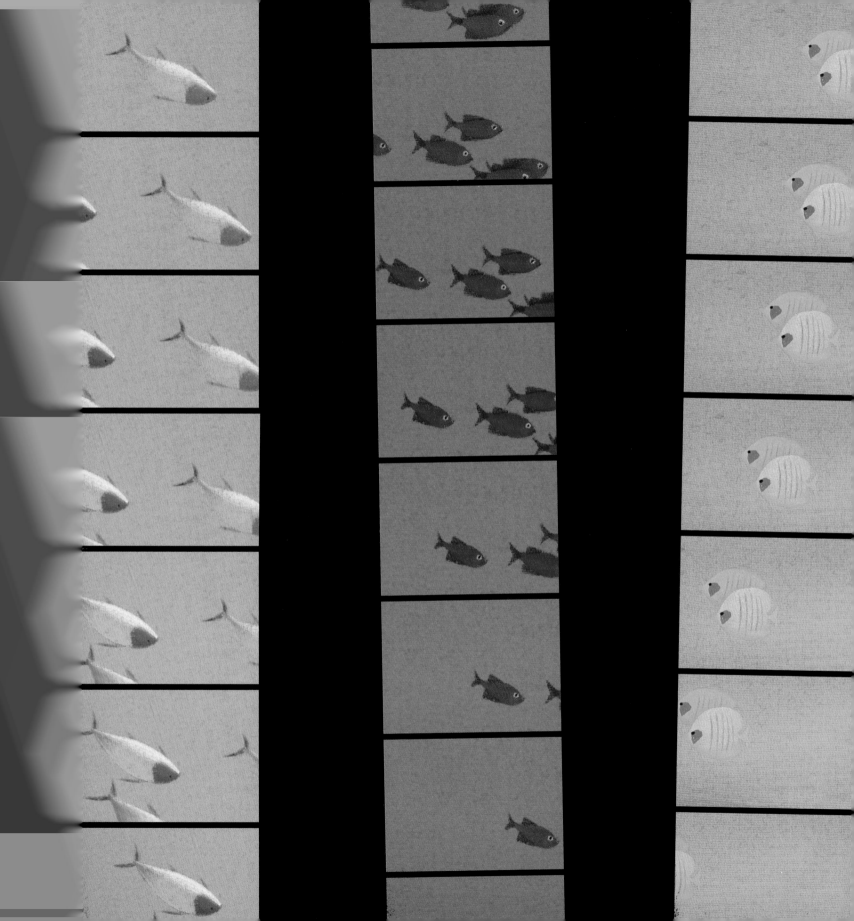

First Chronicle Books LLC paperback
edition, published in 2015. Originally
published in hardcover in 2008 by
Chronicle Books LLC.

Text © 2008 by Jennifer Berne.
Illustrations © 2008 by Éric Puybaret.

ISBN 978–1–4521–4123–7

The Library of Congress has cataloged
the previous edition under ISBN 978–0–8118–6063–5.

Manufactured in China.

MIX
Paper | Supporting
responsible forestry
FSC™ C104723
FSC
www.fsc.org

Design by Sara Gillingham.
Typeset in Pia.
The illustrations in this book were
rendered in acrylic paint on linen.

20 19 18 17 16 15 14

Chronicle Books LLC
680 Second Street, San Francisco, California 94107
www.chroniclekids.com

MANFISH

A Story of Jacques Cousteau

by Jennifer Berne

illustrated by
Éric Puybaret

chronicle books · san francisco

BLES RISING
THROUGH THE SILENCE OF THE SEA,
SILVERY BEADS OF BREATH
FROM A MAN
DEEP, DEEP DOWN
IN A STRANGE AND SHIMMERING OCEAN LAND
OF SWAYING PLANTS AND FANTASTIC CREATURES,
A MANFISH
SWIMMING, DIVING
INTO THE UNKNOWN,
EXPLORING UNDERWATER WORLDS

NO ONE HAD EVER SEEN

AND NO ONE COULD EVER HAVE IMAGINED.

OUR STORY starts many years before, in France, with a little baby boy born under the summer sun.

His parents named him Jacques.

From the very beginning little Jacques loved water—the way it felt on his hands, his face, his body. And water made him wonder. He wondered why ships floated. Why he floated. And why rocks sank.

One day Jacques read a story about a man who hid underwater by breathing through a long tube. Jacques tried it and discovered it was impossible.

He dreamed that someday he would be able to breathe underwater for real.

At night Jacques dreamed he could fly. With the birds, among the clouds, with his arms stretched out like wings.

Jacques spent his days playing, experimenting, and creating. He wrote little books that he illustrated with his own drawings. And he was fascinated by machines. He studied blueprints and built a model of a crane that was as tall as he was, and actually worked.

Movies fascinated Jacques, too. He wanted to know how they were made, how the cameras worked, and how chemicals made pictures appear on the film. Jacques saved his allowance, penny by penny, until he had enough to buy a small home-movie camera. The first thing he did was take it apart and put it back together.

Then he began to film everything around him. He put his brother, cousins, parents, and friends in his movies. He dressed up as a villain with a painted-on mustache, and made some very villainous films. Jacques was always the star, the director, the writer. And usually the cameraman.

WHEN JACQUES FINISHED SCHOOL he joined
the French Navy. His ship sailed all around the world, and
everywhere he went he filmed what he saw.

In China, he filmed men catching fish with their bare hands.
They held their breath underwater for many minutes. Jacques
wondered what that would be like.

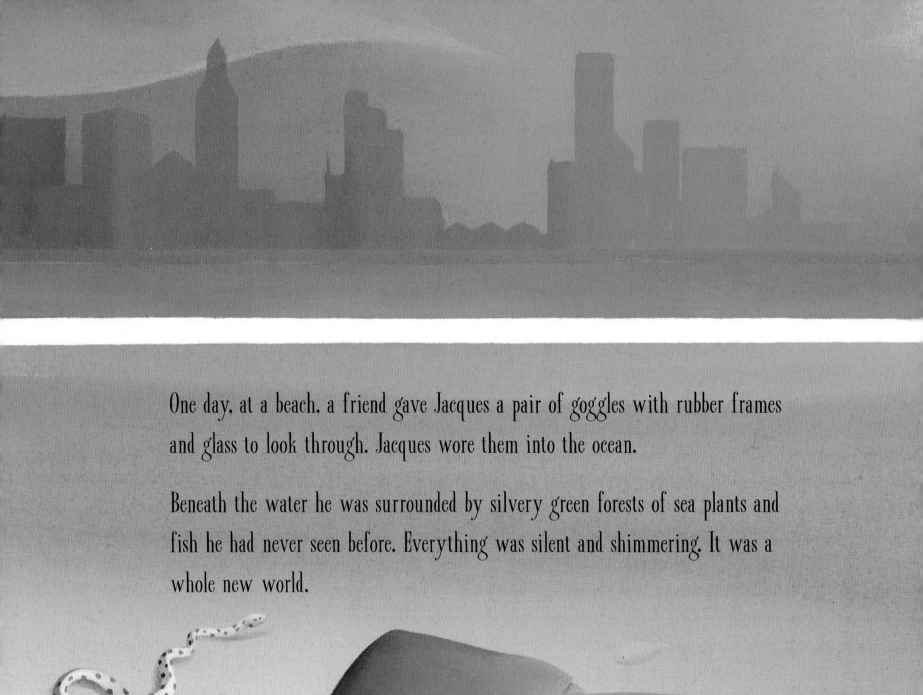

One day, at a beach, a friend gave Jacques a pair of goggles with rubber frames and glass to look through. Jacques wore them into the ocean.

Beneath the water he was surrounded by silvery green forests of sea plants and fish he had never seen before. Everything was silent and shimmering. It was a whole new world.

When he came up he saw cars, people, buildings, and telephone poles. Once again he went below into the magical underwater world. At that moment Jacques knew his life was changed forever. His eyes had been opened to the wonders of the sea.

Jacques and his friends, Philippe and Didi, began to dive together. They experimented to see how long they could stay underwater and how deep they could go.

Jacques created a waterproof case for his camera, to film the amazing kingdom he and his friends were exploring beneath the surface.

They made rubber suits to keep themselves warm and flippers to help them kick better.

But Jacques wanted to stay down longer than just one breath at a time.

He realized he needed to take more air with him, enough air to explore the mysterious depths and vast expanses of the ocean. To swim through the sea as free as a fish.

He wanted to become a manfish.

And he began to work on just how to do it.

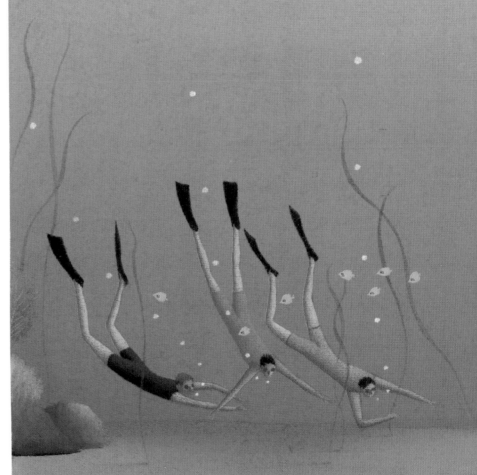

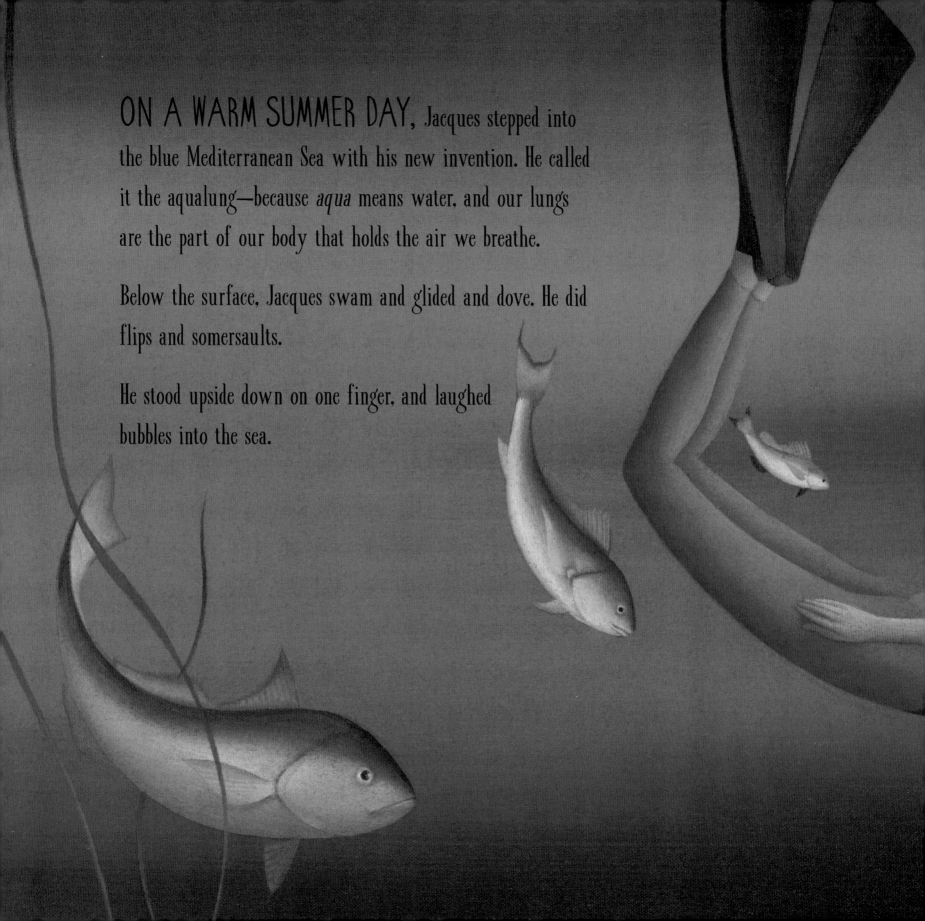

ON A WARM SUMMER DAY, Jacques stepped into
the blue Mediterranean Sea with his new invention. He called
it the aqualung—because *aqua* means water, and our lungs
are the part of our body that holds the air we breathe.

Below the surface, Jacques swam and glided and dove. He did
flips and somersaults.

He stood upside down on one finger, and laughed
bubbles into the sea.

Jacques could breathe beneath the water!

Now he could swim across miles of ocean, his body feeling what only scales had felt, his eyes seeing what only fish had seen. The water made him feel like he was flying. Just like in his dreams.

Jacques had done it. He had become a manfish.

Jacques was ready to explore the oceans of the world. He needed a boat and found a big, old, wooden navy ship named *Calypso*. In a year he turned it from a warship into an explorer's ship.

Jacques, Philippe, and Didi gathered a crew, their aqualungs, their hopes, and their dreams, and set off to explore the inside of the sea, to film a world that no one had ever seen before.

On their journeys, they dove deep into a seascape of plants. Green and purple prickly plants. Red branchy plants. Spongy plants. Wispy, feathery, swaying plants, slow dancing to the rhythms of the sea.

They discovered plants that could feed you. Plants that could poison you. Plants that looked like fish . . . and fish that looked like plants.

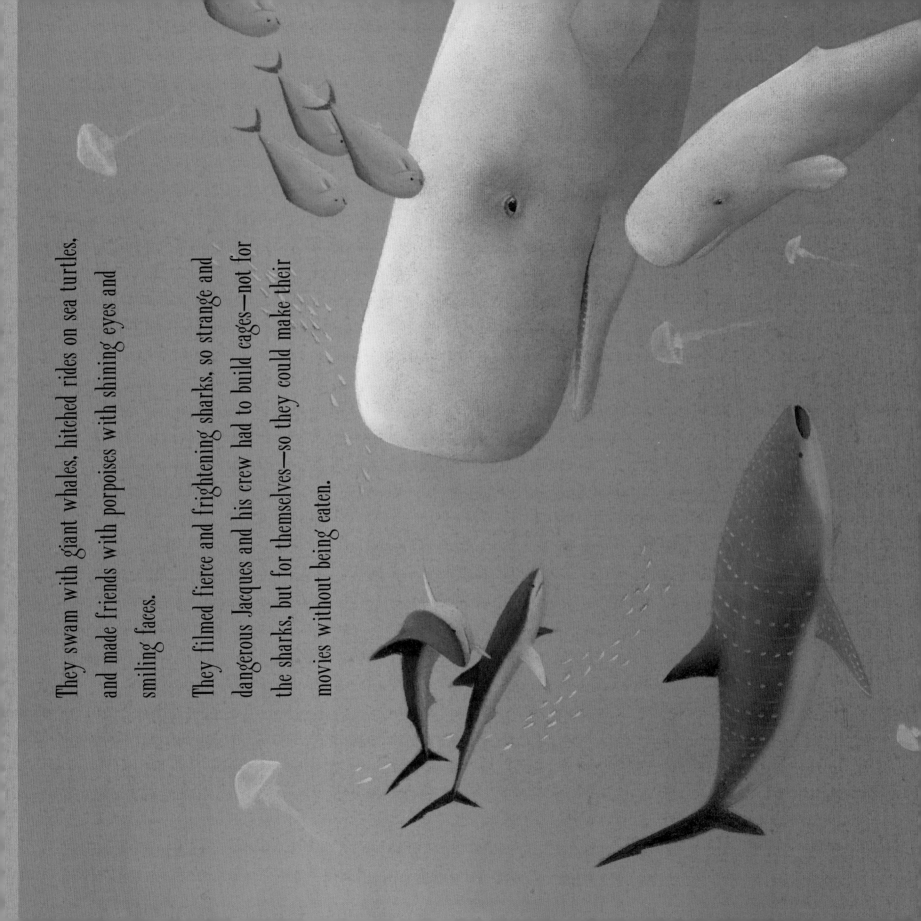

They swam with giant whales, hitched rides on sea turtles, and made friends with porpoises with shining eyes and smiling faces.

They filmed fierce and frightening sharks, so strange and dangerous Jacques and his crew had to build cages—not for the sharks, but for themselves—so they could make their movies without being eaten.

Everywhere the *Calypso* went, Jacques and his crew made films of what they saw. Films that played in movie theaters. Films that played on TV.

Millions of people all over the world discovered the wonders of the sea for the very first time, with Jacques, Philippe, Didi, and their adventurous crew.

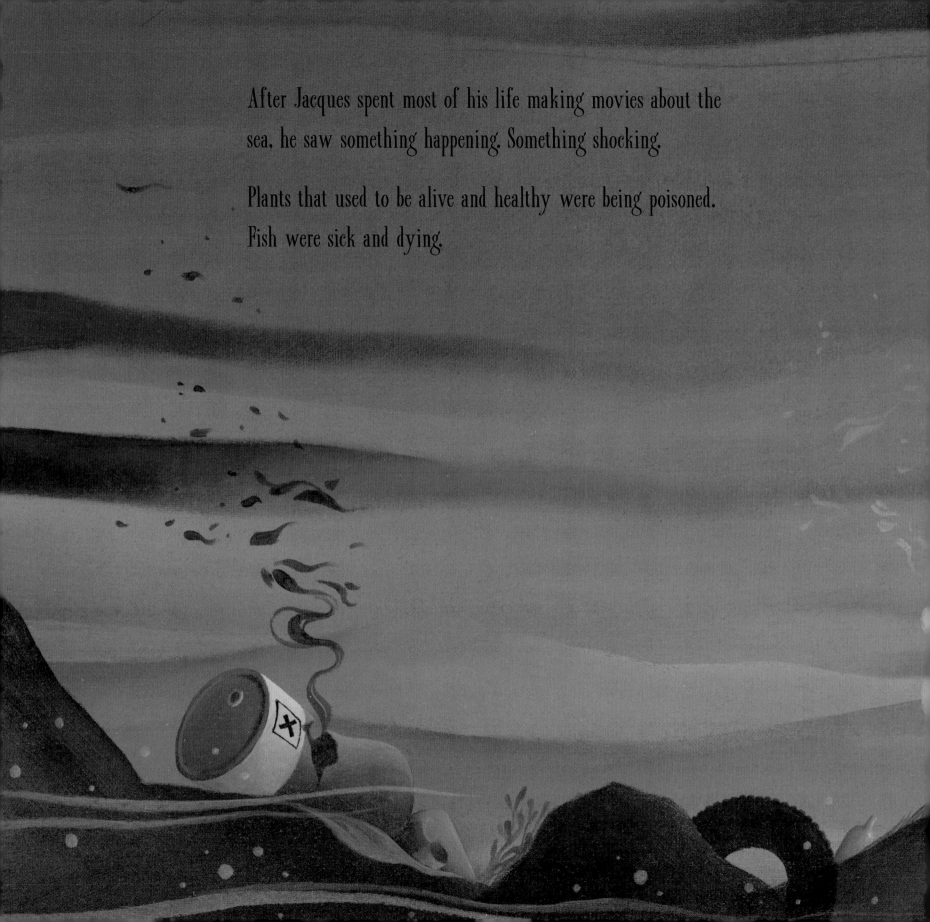

After Jacques spent most of his life making movies about the
sea, he saw something happening. Something shocking.

Plants that used to be alive and healthy were being poisoned.
Fish were sick and dying.

Jacques saw that people, without realizing it, were slowly killing the sea and its creatures, by dumping garbage and poisonous chemicals into the ocean he loved so much.

Jacques knew what he had to do. He had to make movies. Movies to warn people. Movies to save the sea.

Jacques also spoke to presidents. To kings and queens. To people all over the earth. Asking them to help save our oceans, our planet.

And he spoke to children.

Jacques dreamed that someday it would be you, exploring worlds never seen, never imagined. Whole new worlds, silent and shimmering. Worlds that are now yours. To discover. To care for. And to love.

Author's Note

Jacques Cousteau was a remarkable person, truly one–of–a–kind. He was a protector of our planet and its creatures, an inventor, adventurer and explorer, a poetic writer and spokesperson for the sea. He was also an innovative filmmaker and photographer. Most of all, he loved life with a childlike sense of joy and an insatiable curiosity.

His rallying cry wherever he went, whatever he was exploring, was "Il faut aller voir," which translates roughly as "We must go and see for ourselves," which I think is a wonderful way to start just about anything. I feel fortunate for all the time I spent in Jacques Cousteau's world while researching and writing this book.

If you'd like some more Cousteau in your life, here are a few ideas:

JOIN: The Cousteau Society (www.cousteau.org), founded by Jacques Cousteau in 1973 for research, exploration, and education. Join as a "Cousteau Kid," to receive *Cousteau Kids* magazine.

COUSTEAU'S FILMS: Jacques Cousteau made over 115 films. Some are available now from your library or for sale over the Internet, and thanks to the Cousteau Society, almost all of them are available on DVD.

COUSTEAU'S BOOKS: Cousteau wrote over 50 books, full of beautiful pictures and fascinating adventures. His important last book, *The Human, The Orchid, and the Octopus,* was released in the United States in 2010.

THE MARINE WORLD: Most natural history museums have wonderful, informative exhibits about the ocean world. You can also visit ocean research centers or take snorkeling or diving lessons.

CARING FOR OUR PLANET: Cousteau believed that each of us has a responsibility to protect the earth. You can do your part every single day by turning off the water while brushing your teeth, encouraging your family to walk more and ride their bikes, and by turning off the lights when you leave a room. Making an effort to recycle helps, too.

FOLLOWING COUSTEAU'S LEAD: Get a camera and start photographing or filming what interests you. Motivate your family and friends to start caring about the world and its creatures. Above all (I'm sure Cousteau would agree with this): follow your passions, follow your dreams.

J. B.

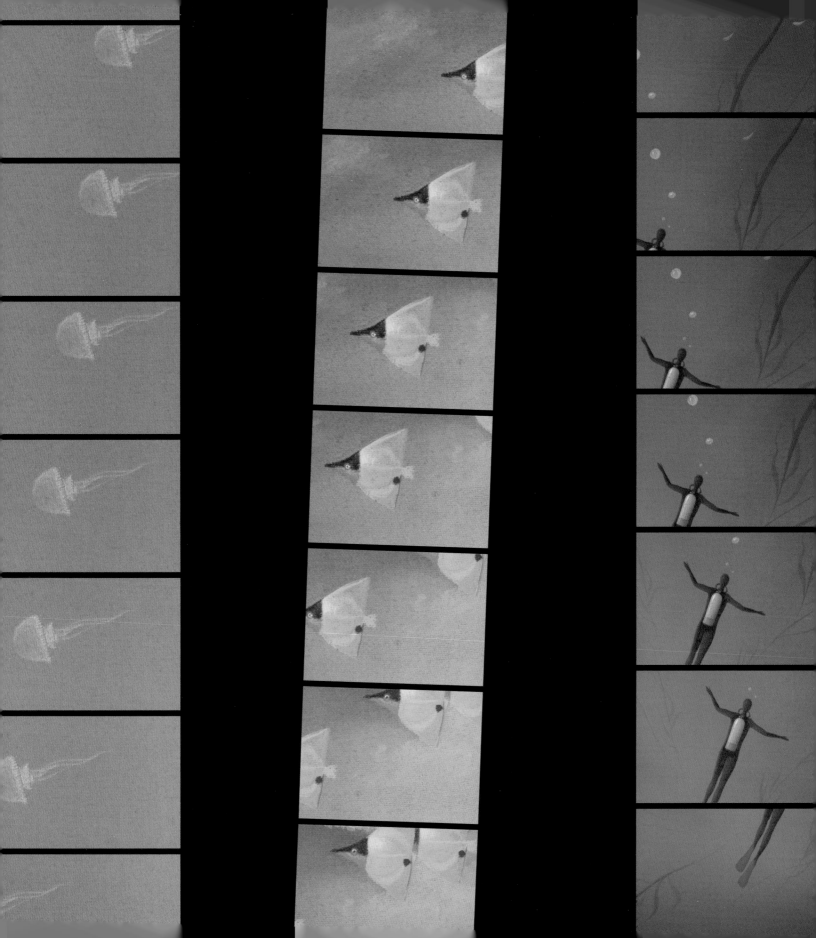

Jennifer Berne grew up in New York City where she was active in dance and theater as a child. As an adult, she and her artist husband, Nick, designed a sailboat, which they sailed from Maine to the Bahamas. Now they spend summers living aboard their boat, cruising Penobscot Bay and beyond.

Jennifer writes about the subjects she loves most—our amazing universe and the people who are passionate about it. She is also the author of the critically acclaimed *On a Beam of Light: A Story of Albert Einstein.*

Award-winning illustrator *Éric Puybaret* was born in Vichy, France. He attended the historic École Nationale Supérieure des Arts Décoratifs in Paris, where he specialized in illustration. He has since illustrated several books for children and is particularly excited to have worked on *Manfish: A Story of Jacques Cousteau* because he spends much of his free time diving and enjoying the sea.